Sista Girlfren'

Francheska Ahmed-Cawthorne

Illustrations by Barbara Brandon

Breaks It Down...
When Mom's
Not Around

A FIRESIDE BOOK
PUBLISHED BY SIMON & SCHUSTER
New York London Toronto Sydney Tokyo Singapore

F

FIRESIDE
Rockefeller Center
1230 Avenue of the Americas
New York, NY 10020

FIRESIDE and colophon are registered trademarks
of Simon & Schuster Inc.

Designed by Jessica Shatan

Manufactured in the United States of America

10 9 8 7 6 5 4 3 2 1

Library of Congress Cataloging-in-Publication Data
Ahmed-Cawthorne, Francheska.
    Sista girlfren' breaks it down— : when Mom's not around /
Francheska Ahmed-Cawthorne : illustrations by Barbara Brandon.
        p.   cm.
    Summary: Advice on everything from dating and boyfriends to
schooling and careers, aimed at African American teenage girls.
    1. Conduct of life.   2. Afro-American girls—Conduct of life.
[1. Conduct of life.]   I. Brandon, Barbara, ill.   II. Title.
BJ1581.2.A34   1996
646.7'00835'2—dc20   96-1913
                                                              CIP
                                                               AC

ISBN 0-684-81899-X

Dedicated to my mother,

EUGENIA "GENIE" L. JACKSON

Who, even though gone, is still "Breakin' It Down!"

Thanks, Mom!

 CONTENTS

Contents

Contents

Contents

◈ INTRODUCTION

After raising six daughters, advising their girlfrens', and counseling hundreds of my college students, I've come to realize you—and most girls—grow up and leave home with very few of your woman questions answered. Not because your mom wouldn't tell you, but because some things are too embarrassing to ask and sometimes parents just don't understand.

So you ask your girlfren', and that's pitiful, because she's also trying to figure life out. I realize what you need is the wisdom of Mom but coming from a girlfren' you can relate to.

So with thoughts and fond memories of my mother and father, a lot of recollection, much applauds from my daughters, and the love and support of my husband—Sista' Girlfren' was created!

Her job:

To make your Mom and Girlfren' one.

Her mission:

To Break It Down when you need advice,

but Mom's Not Around!

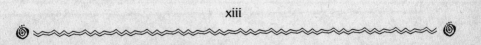

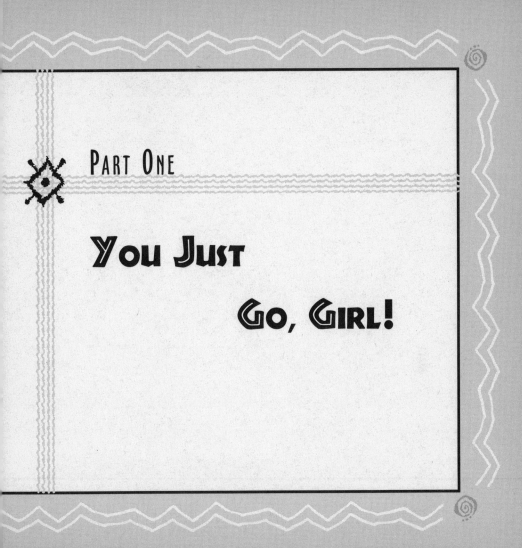

PART ONE

YOU JUST

GO, GIRL!

GO, GIRL!

Girlfren', whenever you start thinkin' you can't succeed,

just remember your first success in life was fighting to breathe.

Yes, the time came when you grew too big for Mom's womb,

and you knew if you stayed it would become your tomb.

So even though you were scared, you really didn't care,

you just started fightin' to get out and breathe

new air.

Life is a constant struggle for success,

so when a new problem comes along,

don't trip:

Think progress!

✕◈✕

Solvin' your own problems is your opportunity to show
how independent you can be when you decide to grow.

✕◈✕

When successful women run into a problem,
they don't bother stressin'.
They just handle their b'ness,
and they keep on steppin'.

✖◈✖

Accomplish somethin' yourself
before you criticize someone else.

BEIN' ALL THAT

To be successful and in demand,

you've got to set goals and make a plan.

Set aside time every day, and work as hard as you can,

and don't be distracted by every party, phone call, or man.

XOX

Success means you did your best at what you tried.

So, if you gave it your all, chill out and enjoy the ride.

XOX

Success will come when, in pursuing your dream,

you let people who can help you join your team.

XOX

Learning somethin' new?

Start with the parts you understand.

Keep workin' at it, and soon you'll be in demand.

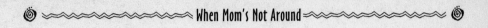
XOX

You want to know the answers?

You betta keep askin' the questions!

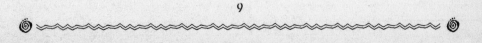

WHO'S IN CHARGE?

When the decision is not up to you,
it's easy to say what *you* would do.

✕◇✕

Blamin' others for *your* problems
implies they have control over you.

And you are a child,

who's not responsible for what you do.

XOX

If you are always blamin' others for your failures,

you'll never succeed.

And you're missin' valuable lessons

that in life you'll later need.

XOX

Followers get what's left.

Leaders get the best.

XOX

Leaders get first choice. Followers get no voice.

XOX

To discover what someone really believes,

don't just listen to what they say, watch their deeds.

XOX

Ninety-nine people will talk about dreams,

only a few people will make theirs come true.

Out of that number,

which one are you!

XOX

Got a bad attitude?

Then when the right opportunity comes along,

you're screwed.

XOX

Drugs may tempt,

but they never force.

When they destroy your life,

you're the source.

13

BEIN' GROWN

Don't burden your childhood with babies
  and strife.
This is the time to enjoy *your* life.

❊❊❊

14

Enjoy your youth while you can.

Cuz if you're older and tryin' to go back and do what

you missed,

Girlfren', you'll just look plain ridiculous.

XOX

You want to be a "G" and act like you're

grown?

Then move out of yo' mama's house and get one of your

own!

XOX

Want to prove you're really grown?

Move out, pay your own bills,

and write your parents a thank-you note.

Thank 'em for your life,

apologize for the bad times;

tell 'em what your goals and plans are,

and explain how much you love them.

Regardless what your relationship has been,

they'll respect your new maturity.

XOX

When you stop askin' and start givin',

your parents can stop providin' and start livin'

XOX

Want to prove you're really grown?

Accept the challenge:

Move out on your own.

XOX

When you start learning from your mistakes, you're beginning to understand what adulthood takes.

YO' J-O-B

Don't complain today about not getting hired,

if in school you didn't study cuz you were too tired.

If designer labels prove you've got it made,

try wearin' "McDonald's," "Wendy's," or "Jack in the Box."

At least for wearin' 'em, you'll be getting paid.

XOX

Drop out of school at fifteen,

by forty you'll still be Burger King's Fry-Queen!

XOX

Ladies who date the criminal type

and say "Girl, he's ALL THAT!"

betta always keep a good job,

cuz that "bail" money can get pretty "Phat!"

XOX

If you want to live large,

then choose a career and talk to who's in charge.

Volunteer to work with her and never come late;

learn all you can, and before long,

bein' well paid will become your lifelong fate!

✕⟡✕

Why wasn't the job given to you?

It could be your attitude adjustment is seriously

overdue.

JUST DO IT!

To guarantee you'll always have a meal,
pick a trade now and learn a skill.

XOX

Take advantage of school while you're young,
so at twenty-two you can afford to hang out and have fun.

23

XOX

If you drop out of school,

you better have awesome talent,

great ambition and drive,

or *very wealthy* folks.

Otherwise, you'll be forever unemployed,

triflin', and always broke.

XOX

Mark was borin', always in his books.

But Jesse was "cool" cuz he hung out with the crooks.

Now at twenty-two, Mark's finished with college and

   his future is bright,

while Jesse is hopin' the police won't raid him tonight!

✖◈✖

Throwin' together your schoolwork just to pass?

The best favor your teacher can do is flunk your sorry @!*!

✖◈✖

On yo' college campus, don't get carried away when
you see all those new guys.

Cuz no matter what they say, the double standard still
applies.

XOX

If you blew off school and didn't care about your career,
at thirty don't whine about being a fast-food cashier.

GETTIN' PAID

Remember the nerds you laughed at while they studied?

Today they're deciding if they should hire you, buddy!

Life is like your bank account,

what you put into it you can take out.

※❖※

You respect Snoop Dogg,

but while you're gangbangin' or collectin' aid,

Snoop is legally handlin' his,

and definitely gettin' paid.

※❖※

28

If you can't pay yo' bills,

you need to learn some earning skills.

For every $100 you make, save $25.

When you're out of work, it'll keep you alive.

Welfare is supposed to be temporary help, not a career.

It's not something to rely on year after year.

PART TWO

SHOULD I
KEEP HIM OR
DUMP HIM?

DATIN' IN THE '90S

If you want a successful man, use your mind.
There are plenty of females offerin' him their
  behind.

Whoever asks for the date should pay.

That, my sista, is the '90s way!

Sleep with him on the first date.

For his next phone call you'll

wait,

wait,

wait!

Always bring money on the dates you don't drive.
In case you want to leave, you've got money for a ride.

If he's cheap on a date,
he'll be cheap as a mate!

If you think you won't want to date him after a year,
then don't encourage him *now*, my dear.

If he sounds strange on the phone,
definitely don't invite him into your home.

Gettin' with a man for what he's got—
He'll love, cherish, and share it with you—NOT!

Young men like to explore,

try their rap,

and get those digits same as you.

So ladies,

while you're still hangin' out,

accept that he will too!

∾

If he's stingy with his money,

he'll be stingy with his love.

And unless that changes,

that's not something your love can rise above.

☉

Girlfren', stop givin' your heart and soul away

to just any ol' man who happens along.

Because it's your heart you must listen to,

in order to decide with whom you belong.

A GOOD MAN

You know you've found the right man when you both
   like spendin' time together
and you can't stop smilin' around each other.
You already feel great about yourself, but he makes you
   feel even better

and you both feel empty when you're apart.

That's when you know, you have each other's heart.

∽

A good man lookin' for a woman judges her by
what's in her head.

Boys on the prowl only wonder whether she's good in
bed.

∽

When he's ready to be yo' man,

he won't even notice another girl,

cuz you'll be the most important woman in his world.

How do you know if he's a good man?

A Check List:

   He treats all the women in his life with respect

   He's not stingy

   Has no dangerous vices

Loves a challenge

Is willing to learn new things

Likes bein' him

Wants help developing his potential

Has his own (legal) income

Is flexible

Does his best at whatever he tries

Yo' man is good if he fits most of these traits.

If yo' man fits them all, he's not just good, he's great!

IT'S ALL GOOD

Yo' man needs to feel needed,

he wants to provide.

So give him some choices

that he must decide.

Give him a role in your life he can play,

and you'll see how much he adds to each day.

43

Thank him each time

with yo' feminine charms,

and you'll have a happy man in your arms.

He'll work like a dog for your smiles and kisses.

He'll fulfill almost all your desires and wishes.

But of course there are limits to what he can earn,

So, Girlfren', don't ask for more than he can return!

∞

You know what keeps a man attracted to you?

The way you treat him and your personality, too!

∽

Remember to say "I love you," and tell each other why.
So your relationship won't go stale on you, peter out,
   and die.

∽

Girlfren', you're not the only one who enjoys being
   pampered, romanced, complimented, and pursued.
This treatment has the same effect on yo' man's
   attitude.

☙❧

Don't wait to tell him the truth cuz you're afraid how
   he'll feel;
cuz he's gonna feel worse, when he finds out the real
   deal.
So find a good time and tell him all you've
   concealed.
You might be surprised at what is revealed.

☙❧

How do you keep a man?
By learnin' about yourself, everything that you possibly can.

Men learn to be better men from women they've known.
Women learn to be better women from men they've loved.

๛

Want to keep your relationship alive!
Don't forget to romance each other just like in the
courtship.

๛

You want to teach your man how to treat you right!
Show him great appreciation when he does what you
like.

CREEPIN'

Wouldn't you rather be the woman of your own
house
than the girl he plays with when he's not with his
spouse?
So don't settle for "quickie" breaks from his wife.
Girlfren', you deserve a full-time man in your life!

෧

Leave yo' fren's man alone till she sets him free.

Then let her know it's him you want to see.

By your girlfren's reaction you should be able

   to see

whether or not it was meant to be.

෧

Okay, she stole your man,

now what'cha gonna do?

Fight her?

Make a scene?

Embarrass her (and you too)?

If you want to come out on top,

forget all that.

Next time you see them together,

smile, and thank her for gettin' that

weak boy outa your way.

And don't sit around stressin',

get out there and play,

cuz if those two conspired to do this,

they'll both get their day!

51

Are you being taken for granted by yo' man!

Listen up, Girlfren', these things you must understand.

If you're so wrapped up in him

you've forgotten your own dreams,

then fixin' this is not as hard as it seems.

He fell in love with the woman that you were,

so go back and be the new improved her.

I guarantee, once you get yo' priorities together,

he'll get excited again and want you forever.

DON'T GET MAD, GET SMART!

Got a problem with a man?

Don't get mad, get smart.

Do the opposite of what is expected of your part.

Cuz when you get mad,

your weaknesses unfold.

And from that point on,

you can be controlled.

ဢ

The winner is the one that's too smart to fight!

ဢ

If you want to win the upper hand,

make your point by calmly discussin'.

Cuz the battle is lost

by the one who starts cussin'.

∞

Two females fightin' over one man!

Wow, you've both been had.

Cuz he's tricked you both into forgettin'

it's at him you should be mad.

∞

When you stop arguin'

and say somethin' positive to yo' man.

You'll be surprised to learn

you've got the upper hand.

If you're always worried about other women

takin' yo' men,

You gotta admit, that's pretty extreme!

Maybe it's time to boost your own self-esteem.

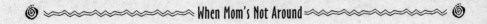

Girlfren', if he was really yo' man, he wouldn't be
    noticing me,
cuz a real man's not confused about where his attention
    should be.

Ladies who are always trying to take yo' man
are really just jealous of the attention you command.

DUMP HIM!

If he acts like a dog,
kick him out till he's house-trained!

∞

You say all the men you attract are dogs,

then, Girlfren', you need to check yourself.

Maybe it's time to change *your* tune

so a better class of men you'll be attracting soon.

∽

You say your man's a dog and he'll sleep with
  anything.

But, Girlfren', you're still datin' him,

so what are you *really* saying?

If yo' man breaks up with you,

get a grip and move on.

Cuz you're gonna get dissed

if you keep holdin' on.

If he's supposed to be yo' man, he'll come back.

And in the meantime, Girlfren',

get yo' self-esteem intact.

You say yo' man was plucked from you like a

flower.

But I say, Girlfren', you don't know how to use your

power.

Once you understand your strengths,

and learn how to work 'em too!

Oh, Please!!!!

No man or woman can take anything from you!

If yo' man up and leaves you,

don't sit aroun' poutin' and feelin' bad.

Cuz by now you've learned you'll survive

even those times when you're sad.

And this is the lesson you need to learn:

to become the confident woman

no man will burn.

BUCK WILD!

Listen up, Girlfren'

When it comes to sex, here's what you need to know:

Young men become interested in sex

way before they can handle

commitment and responsibility.

And, Girlfren', if you can't teach him these

 two,

then he's not ready for sex,

and neither are you!

Another thing is,

young ladies like to be held,

told they're pretty,

and loved.

But a young man will say anything

for a chance to sink his sub!

So girls, how do you solve this?

What should you do?

Just remember, as unfair as it seems,

maturity and responsibility are up to you!

Cuz young men will remain boys as long as you let 'em—

and if you're not careful,

you'll be the one sittin' up expectin'!

So ladies it's okay to hug and kiss for a while,

but wait 'till you're both responsible enough

before goin' "Buck Wild"!

How do you know if you're ready for sex?
When you're sure you can handle whatever happens
   next.

Each guy you sleep with is the potential father of your
   child.
Look at him good, then think about that for a while.

A kiss is a pleasant reminder that two heads are better than one.

∾

Havin' a lot of sex and having a good relationship are two entirely different things.

∾

The best gifts come wrapped up = Use condoms!

PART THREE

YOU'VE GOTTA
RESPECT YO'SELF

BUSTIN' OUT

Bustin' out of your clothes?

Don't get a bigger size.

Get into a routine of fruits, water, and exercise.

If fast food is all you eat,

eventually your stomach will hang out over your feet.

❖ ❖

Women who don't eat cuz they think thin is wise

are destroying their brain cells along with their thighs.

❖ ❖

It's the fat in your food

that makes you fat in your stomach, hips, and thighs.

Keep eatin' all that fat,

and you'll be buying a bigger size.

❁ ❁

Your body gets an attitude when you keep

dissin' it.

❁ ❁

Eat fruits, vegetables, and foods labeled "Fat Free,"

and when you turn thirty, you will thank me.

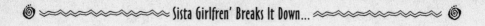

❖ ❖

Get healthy, not super thin:

It lasts longer.

❖ ❖

Rule of Thumb:

Worried about your weight?

Read the fat content on the label.

If it's over 12 fat grams,

take it off your table.

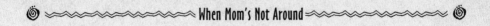

❖ ❖

When you stop takin' care of your body,
it will stop takin' care of you!

❖ ❖

Once you lose your health,
you've lost your greatest wealth.

75

DRESS TO IMPRESS

 Jus' cuz it's in style

doesn't mean it fits *your* profile.

❋ ❋

 Dress to impress,

not to show all yo' b'ness.

76

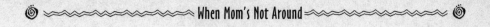

Women have beautiful bodies

designed to bring men to their knees.

So, Girlfren', it's up to you,

to decide just how much he sees.

Start dressin' sexy when you're only thirteen,

and by twenty you're the worn-out female every man's

already seen.

※ ※

All dressed up, lookin' clean and neat,
don't leave the house with dirty shoes and ashy feet.

※ ※

Invest in one nice black outfit,
buy silver or gold accessories
and black heels to match.
When a special event comes up,
no problem, don't sweat!

78

You've got a little somethin'
that's always a good bet.

❂ ❂

If it jiggles, it shouldn't show.

❂ ❂

Your gorgeous body a man don't have to see,
cuz your strut makes him imagine how sexy it
   must be.

Then, if he's curious, he'll have to come to you straight,
and ask you politely if you'll go out on a date.

❖ ❖

Always buy at least two pairs of stockings when you
   shop.
If you get a run, you'll have a swap.

❖ ❖

Makeup and sex don't make you grown.
They just make young girls welfare prone.

YO' HAIR

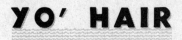

Good hair = Hair you can wear in any style, straight, curly, waved, or braided.

But any style kept toooo long no longer looks good, but faded.

Go to hairdressers early mornings in the middle of the
week.

They'll treat you better and you'll get the attention you
seek.

Yo' hair is there just for added flair.

It's the total you that should make men stare.

Don't spend so much time on your hair

that your mind and body can't even

compare.

TAKE A WHIFF!

The best dressed woman in any room has the warmest smile,
the most confidence, and is well groomed.

✷ ✷

Brush your teeth and check yo' breath.

You want him close,

not comatose!

That time of the month = Your week to relax and take
   care of you.

It's your monthly reminder that you should renew.

Don't think for one second that by putting on perfume

you get to skip the shower.

Don't ya know funk has the

stronger odor power?

RESPECT YO'SELF

Feelin' sick?

Relax, calm yourself with a hot bath,

nice music, and something good to read.

That'll eliminate the stress

 so you can get some of the relief you need.

When you're hurt and feeling real bad,

there's a lesson in your pain to be had.

Think about how the pressure and stress came on.

When you figure that out, the pain will soon be

   gone.

Who makes you happy?

Think about *that* for a while.

Then spend your time with those people

who like makin' you smile.

❖ ❖

Don't be jealous of what another woman's got.

Find somethin' about you that makes you hot!

❖ ❖

Don't say I'll be happy when . . .

Be happy now so your life can begin.

89

The best person to follow is in your own mirror.

She's always been there for you.

Always will be, too.

Don't let someone else's bad opinion of you become
your own!

90

When three different people give you the exact

same advice,

it's time, Girlfren', for you to think twice.

❊ ❊

When he says he can't resist her,

he's talking about a wise and feminine sista.

YOU'VE GOT SOUL!

Your soul is the only thing you keep when
   you die,
so don't sell it just to keep some guy.

❁ ❁

The dreams that you feel you must pursue

are messages your soul is sending you.

❖ ❖

If you listen to your heart and pursue your dreams,

you'll discover your life's purpose

and boost your esteem.

And anyone who knows you

will look at you and say

you're the brightest person they've seen that day!

If you keep chasin' a dream

and stay at it,

pretty soon you'll catch it.

Live every day like it's your last day on earth,

and you'll get to see what your life is really worth.

To find happiness, you sometimes must risk pain,

but then happiness will be yours to gain.

❖ ❖

Your greatest strength is bein' feminine.

Feminine means usin' your mind before your tongue.

Feminine means wisely handlin' everyone.

It means softness is your tool—

and you make everyone comfortable while you

   quietly rule.

95

PART FOUR

WHO'S REALLY GOT YO' BACK?

YO' FAMILY

You say yo' gang is yo' family, that's funny!

Then why do you keep goin' home for food, a bed, and

bail money?

Your family exists to teach you something about life;

and while the lessons can be sometimes mean

and sometimes sweet,

regardless, it is your responsibility to learn

and then stand up on your own two feet.

6̄6̄6̄

Your family is there to give you moral support,

not to be dragged back and forth with you to court.

6̄6̄6̄

Homeys know your problems;
families help you solve them.

When you cry to yo' mom about your fights with
   yo' man,
remember to tell her when the fight's resolved,
otherwise Mom's still gonna be holdin' a grudge,
cuz she'll think you're *still* being dogged.

You glorify the elders of the motherland,

but treat your own parents like you don't give a

damn!

Why wait til' they're dead and out of sight

before you decide to start treatin' *them* right!

⊠⊠⊠

Your parents wiped your butt when you were small.

So make sure you take care of them when they need

y'all.

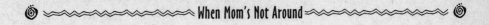

Common sense often comes
when Mom and Dad dry up the funds.

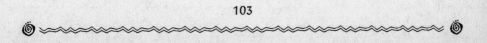

YO' MAMA SAID

Right now, you think your mom's too negative,

her punishments are too strong.

She's always there talkin' 'bout what you did wrong.

But when you become an adult,

you'll say, "just fine."

104

Cuz with your own kids you'll be using the same
  lines.

***

If I do somethin' you don't like,
find a way of your own.

***

Honey, I'll always love you,
but I may not always like what you do.

Let me tell you my life stories before I'm gone.

So when you have children you can pass them on!

When you let yo' man make *all* your decisions,

he's gonna make sure they suit *his* visions.

HAVIN' BABIES

When you talk bad to your kids, or tell 'em to "Go to
   Hell!"
you're creating the future criminals you'll be visitin' in
   jail.

 G irlfren', rememba all the changes you put yo' mama
 through?
When *you* have babies they'll do it doubly to you!

 D on't have babies till you can give them all they need—
responsible parents, a home, and the guidance to
 succeed.

Babies learn about life from watchin' you.

So, Girlfren', pay close attention to everything

   you do.

Every cute baby grows up to be somebody.

Since they can't forever rely on their looks,

make sure they learn what's inside of books.

Who's really all that?

Not the gangbanger who gets respect with guns.

Not the boy who makes a baby and runs.

No, it's the single mom

who can still raise successful daughters and sons.

Girls, when you have a baby that you can't afford,

you make the government yo' man.

And we both know you didn't lay-up with Uncle Sam.

HOMEYS

A true girlfren' knows when you're doin' bad
and will tell you the truth,
even if it makes you mad.

If all you ever think about is you,

then when you really need a friend,

no one will be there for you.

Don't be yo' fren's problem solver

if you don't even try to solve your own.

You don't like her

but won't tell her why?

Then don't keep hangin' with her
and behind her back, laugh and lie.

Don't throw away a girlfren'
for just any ol' guy,
You can keep both in your life,
you just need to try.

Don't always have yo' sistafren'
tagging along when you're out on a date.

She's there for *you*,

NOT your mate.

<hr>

Tell all yo' b'ness to a fren',

sooner or later you'll hear it again.

<hr>

On a special evening,

keep all yo' frens and their problems out of your house,

cuz *his* patience during a romantic evening

they will surely douse.

ROOMIES

Good frens are great to have aroun',

but they usually make the worst roommates in town!

Want to lose a good fren'?

Move one in.

Bad credit = Bad roommate!

Clean up your own mess.

Your mom doesn't live at your address.

Post schedules, with everyone's name for each bill

and the amount that's due.

And put it where everyone can see it,

so they can't say they never knew.

⟨⟨⟨

If there's three roomies and one's a guy,

don't try to get with him,

and I'll tell you why.

You'll divide your home, and when rent comes due,

I guarantee neither of your roommates will come

   through!

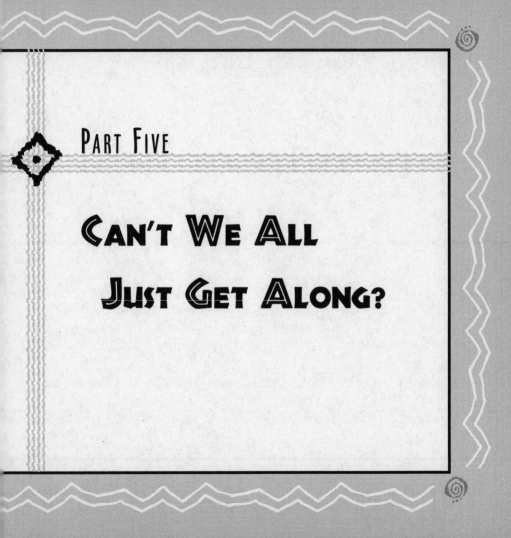

PART FIVE

CAN'T WE ALL JUST GET ALONG?

GOT A 'TUDE?

Y‌ou want to be loved, respected, and pursued?
Then don't be loud, easy, filthy mouthed, and rude.

❋ ❋ ❋

If you're always puttin' others down,

when *you* fall no one will come around!

✳ ✳ ✳

When your life is over,

and all is said and done,

it's not who you were that counts

but how you treated everyone.

✳ ✳ ✳

Rollin' your eyes when an attractive woman walks in

only makes you look bad in comparison.

A confident woman would compliment her,

or at least be civil,

because she would see in her an equal,

not the need to compete.

# # #

Okay, you've got Big Breasts and Butt.

Now what?

✳ ✳ ✳

Anyone who has the power to put you in check,
whether you like 'em or not,
you better show them R-E-S-P-E-C-T!

✳ ✳ ✳

If your car is what makes you who you are,
you're not very much.

✳ ✳ ✳

You can't take a break from doin' nothin'.

WHAT GOES AROUN'...

Dis . . .

You'll get dissed back!

What goes aroun',

comes back on you like a motha!

# # #

People will treat you the way you let 'em.

If someone's dissin' you, you betta' check 'em.

# # #

Men cheat and we help 'em!

Every time we get with another woman's man,

we're sayin',

"About other women, We Don't Give a Damn!"

# # #

If we'd start respect each other's space,

men wouldn't have other women to embrace.

✳ ✳ ✳

Show men you respect yourself

 and other women too.

Tell him you wouldn't do to him

what you wouldn't want done to you.

✳ ✳ ✳

If you think you're nothin',

so will everyone else.

COLOR LINES—

FREE YO' MIND!

acism:

Insecure people spreading bad rumors about a
  group.

No one challenges them,

so everyone's their dupe.

The targeted group can't defend itself from
   the lies.
and that, Girlfren', is how *racism* survives.

✳ ✳ ✳

When it comes right down to it,
racism and jealousy are really the same.
It's all about insecure people finding others to
   blame.

✳ ✳ ✳

No race is superior,

each one has worth.

And when Americans start respectin' each other,

we'll have the "baddest" country on earth.

✻ ✻ ✻

Hold up!

First off, how is it your loss when he dates outside his

own race!

Unless you were his wife,

he wasn't gonna get with you in the first place.

YOU GOT PLAYED!

It's your fear that will keep you down—

so toss it off and turn it aroun'.

✳ ✳ ✳

Fear can make you weak and insecure.

It can even make you stay in a violent relationship you

shouldn't endure.

✳ ✳ ✳

When you lose the confidence to try

somethin' new,

it's cuz you've let fear overpower you.

Don't let your fear keep you stuck where you are,

try to remember that in this life

you're the star.

❋❋❋

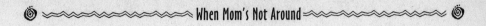

When you can't get your life in gear,
look what's stopping you:
Your fear!

❋❋❋

You think he beats you out of love—WRONG!
He beats you out of shame.
Cuz he's scared of life so he's using you to blame.
Yes, he needs counselin', he needs self-esteem;

what he doesn't need is to keep punchin' you out of your
   dreams.

Your face can't help him, not your back, nor your love.

Make him get help

before he can deserve your love.

SELL-OUTS

Sell-outs aren't people you want to hang out with or meet.

They're criminals who shoot kids

and sell drugs on the street.

They're pimps, thieves, and child abusers.

Or deadbeat dads and drug users.

Sell-outs are people who hate their own race.

And tell their own people "Stay in your place."

They're dangerous people,

we don't need them aroun',

cuz they betray everyone

and bring their community down.

❖ CONCLUSION

Well, ladies, if you've read this far, I'm proud of you because you've completed the first step in finding your own answers.

This is exciting to me because it proves what I've already known about each one of you: You can finish what you start; you don't whine about your problems, you look for answers; and you respect yourself enough to look for ways to be better.

Let me tell you a little secret: The answers you're looking for are already inside you. You see snatches of them every day—in your smile, your heart, your beliefs, your conscience, your desires, dreams, and in your likes and dislikes.

And as long as you're serious about becoming the "All That Woman" that's inside you, she will keep helping you.

So ask your questions, but understand the answers. Enjoy being young so you can enjoy being an adult.

Learn everything about yourself and improve what you don't like. Listen to your heart and conscience when they're telling you no! And keep loving your positive self.

Lastly, Girlfren', as long as you keep growing, and enjoying your youth, I'll keep telling you all that I know and am still finding out.

SISTA GIRLFREN'

aka

Francheska Ahmed-Cawthorne

❊ ACKNOWLEDGMENTS

First, I want to thank my parents, Art and Genie Jackson, for giving me enough growing room to make my mistakes, and enough love and guidance to learn from those mistakes.

I also want to thank my three handsome brothers and two special sisters for providing support for each other and being the best examples of what brothers and sisters should be.

Secondly, to my wonderful husband Herb Cawthorne, who made it possible for me to finally put these words on paper: You've also helped me discover the loving woman inside myself. Thanks to you, I now understand what heaven is; it's when you find and marry your Soul Mate. I'm in heaven!

To all my children, natural and borrowed; Maliha and Imani, Sahirah, Rajah, Tunisia, Elise, Alena, Jon, Victor, Lamont, and everyone else who calls me Mom. Thank you for being every type of personality known to (wo)man. You've all kept me on my toes and given me the opportunity to give and receive and keep up with young ideas.

Also, to all my students, thanks for the experience, and for all you've taught me.

And to all my friends, thank you for letting me analyze your lives and grow with you. Thanks for your encouragement, counseling, conversations, disagreements, laughter, tears, secrets, business ventures, Number 8 discipline, and to Maxine for my sanity and my hair.

Finally, I want to thank my coaches and those who inspired me. First, Laurie Bernstein, who I'm sure I knew in my previous life, because she understood Sista Girlfren' so quickly and offered her a home at Simon & Schuster. Thank you for turning a rough draft into a book. And Annie Hughes: Your gentle voice kept me motivated when I felt like I couldn't go on. Thank you.

My inspirations came from Genie Jackson, who wrote lyrics, melodies, plays, proposals, and dramas up until her last day. From Gloria Naylor and her *The Women of Brewster Place* because she raised a family and then became a published writer. From Salt 'n' Pepa, who sing about positive images for women. From Mary McLeod Bethune and Marian Wright Edelman, who both devoted their lives to making children's lives better. And finally, I get my courageous inspiration from Harriet Tubman. I believe we should set aside a day to honor her, because this sista had a mission and set high goals, and she did whatever was necessary to carry them out. And, Girlfren', she wasn't distracted by any "party, phone call, or man." It was her strong will and her unshaking determination that made the impossible possible. And me free to write this book.

Sista Girlfren'

aka

Francheska Ahmed-Cawthorne